Signs of Jesus Coming

Chris A. Legebow

ISBN-13: 978-1-988914-07-7

DEDICATION

To all the excellent Bible teachers, pastors, evangelists, apostles, and prophets who have helped me gain understanding and wisdom of the return of Jesus through the Holy Spirit.

CONTENTS

ACKNOWLEDGMENTS

All scripture taken from Biblegateway.com
Modern English Version (MEV)

1 SIGNS OF JESUS COMING: INTRODUCTION

Jesus promised that He would return. He ascended up into heaven visibly in front of over 500 witnesses on the Mount of Olives. He had risen from the dead. He appeared on the earth over 40 days after his resurrection in a resurrected body. He had the nail prints in the hands and feet and scar on his side from the piercing sword. The people began asking about the coming of his kingdom perhaps believing since he had risen from the dead he would fulfill all Messianic prophecy and begin to reign in Jerusalem as king. As He talked with the them he started ascending into heaven. His parting words were instructions:

Acts 1: 4 Being assembled with them, He commanded them, "Do not depart from Jerusalem, but wait for the promise of the Father, of which you have heard from Me.[a] 5 For John baptized with water, but you shall be baptized with the Holy Spirit not many days from now."

6 So when they had come together, they asked Him, "Lord, will You at this time restore the kingdom to Israel?"

7 He said to them, "It is not for you to know the times or the dates, which the Father has fixed by His own authority. 8 But you shall receive power when the Holy Spirit comes upon you. And you shall be My witnesses in Jerusalem, and in all Judea and Samaria, and to the ends of the earth."

9 When He had spoken these things, while they looked, He was taken up. And a cloud received Him from their sight.

Before he died, Jesus had told the disciples he would die and be resurrected and that he would leave them, but he also comforted them with his words:

John 14: 3 And if I go and prepare a place for you, I will come again and receive you to Myself, that where I am, you may be also. 4 You know where

I am going, and you know the way."

John 14: 5 Thomas said to Him, "Lord, we do not know where You are going. How can we know the way?"

6 Jesus said to him, "I am the way, the truth, and the life. No one comes to the Father except through Me. 7 If you had known Me, you would have known My Father also. From now on you do know Him and have seen Him."

10 While they looked intently toward heaven as He ascended, suddenly two men stood by them in white garments. 11 They said, "Men of Galilee, why stand looking toward heaven? This same Jesus, who was taken up from you to heaven, will come in like manner as you saw Him go into heaven."

It was clear that he was not answering him about the reign of the Messiah. The angels made it clear that the same Jesus they saw ascending up into the clouds was going to return as he promised. He had his resurrected physical body but also was able to ascend into the heavens. Jesus had triumphed over death and was evidence that their faith in him was eternal life.

He promised the Holy Spirit. The Holy Spirit's coming to them was new. No one had been baptized in the Holy Spirit. Of these disciples, 120 waited in the Upper room at Jerusalem until the moving of the Holy Spirit. They waited and prayed not knowing what would occur but believing in Jesus words.

Acts 2: 2 Suddenly a sound like a mighty rushing wind came from heaven, and it filled the whole house where they were sitting. 3 There appeared to them tongues as of fire, being distributed and resting on each of them, 4 and they were all filled with the Holy Spirit and began to speak in other tongues, as the Spirit enabled them to speak.

The baptism of the Holy Spirit – or this miracle of supernatural praising and worshipping God in different languages was a fulfillment of the promise. Jesus had spoken to the disciples discreetly telling them he most certainly would not leave them without a comforter. He would send the Holy Spirit. I am sure the disciples did not understand what He was talking about until it was completely fulfilled. He promised to send the Spirit.

John 14: 15 "If you love Me, keep My commandments. 16 I will pray the

Father, and He will give you another Counselor, that He may be with you forever: 17 the Spirit of truth, whom the world cannot receive, for it does not see Him, neither does it know Him. But you know Him, for He lives with you, and will be in you. 18 I will not leave you fatherless. I will come to you. 19 Yet a little while and the world will see Me no more. But you will see Me. Because I live, you will live also. 20 On that day you will know that I am in My Father, and you are in Me, and I am in you. 21 He who has My commandments and keeps them is the one who loves Me. And he who loves Me will be loved by My Father. And I will love him and will reveal Myself to him."

25 "I have spoken these things to you while I am still with you. 26 But the Counselor, the Holy Spirit, whom the Father will send in My name, will teach you everything and remind you of all that I told you. 27 Peace I leave with you. My peace I give to you. Not as the world gives do I give to you. Let not your heart be troubled, neither let it be afraid.

First take note that Jesus said these things about the Holy Spirit:

1.   Only believers in Jesus would receive the Holy Spirit.
2.   The Holy Spirit would bring comfort.
3.   The Holy Spirit would come to live with them.
4.   The Holy Spirit would teach them
5.   The Holy Spirit would remind them of all Jesus had spoken.
6.   The Holy Spirit would bring peace.

Jesus mentioned the role of the Holy Spirit while he talked with his disciples.

John 16: 7 Nevertheless I tell you the truth: It is expedient for you that I go away. For if I do not go away, the Counselor will not come to you. But if I go, I will send Him to you. 8 When He comes, He will convict the world of sin and of righteousness and of judgment: 9 of sin, because they do not believe in Me; 10 of righteousness, because I am going to My Father, and you will see Me no more; 11 and of judgment, because the ruler of this world stands condemned.

13 But when the Spirit of truth comes, He will guide you into all truth. For He will not speak on His own authority. But He will speak whatever He hears, and He will tell you things that are to come. 14 He will glorify Me, for He will receive from Me and will declare it to you. 15 All that the Father has is Mine. Therefore, I said that He will take what is Mine and will declare it to you.

The Holy Spirit would be righteous and reprove the world of sin. The Holy Spirit would reveal righteousness. The Holy Spirit would speak righteous judgement. The Holy Spirit would magnify Jesus. With the coming of the Holy Spirit came an unction in the disciples. They were praising God and speaking with the glory of God visibly upon them. They were so overwhelmed by the Holy Spirit's presence that it compelled them into the streets below where they spoke openly praising God in other languages in front of thousands of pilgrims who had gathered to celebrate the feast of tabernacles. What occurred is that thousands of people wanted to know what was occurring. Peter preached a message of repentance using Jesus and the Messianic prophecies he fulfilled. The people were moved and were willing to receive God.

Acts 2: 38 Peter said to them, "Repent and be baptized, every one of you, in the name of Jesus Christ for the forgiveness of sins, and you shall receive the gift of the Holy Spirit. 39 For the promise is to you, and to your children, and to all who are far away, as many as the Lord our God will call."

40 With many other words he testified and exhorted them, saying, "Be saved from this perverse generation." 41 Then those who gladly received his word were baptized, and that day about three thousand souls were added to them.

The Church

What occurred was the multiplication of the church from hundreds of people to thousands of people. It had begun. It was the beginning of the age of the Church. From there, the gospel spread throughout Israel and later through the apostle Paul and Peter and others from the Jerusalem Church it was spread into Asia and Europe as Jesus had commanded. It has been over 2000 years since this occurred. At first, I believe the Christians hoped that the second coming of Christ would occur in their lives. Throughout the past 2000 years many false prophets and teachers arose giving a day and hour of Christ's return.

These false teachers may have been well meaning but what they especially were, was deceived. Jesus clearly told them no man would know the day or the hour of his coming. He confessed that He Himself did not know (while He was living on the earth). The emphasis is that anyone who tells you he or she knows of a certainty that Jesus is coming on this particular day is deceived. It is doubtful that they would knowingly try to lie to you to get you to believe a lie. Certainly though, they are preaching and teaching deception by not heeding Jesus' words.

Matthew 24: 36 "Concerning that day and hour no one knows, not even the angels of heaven, but My Father only. 37 As were the days of Noah, so will be the coming of the Son of Man. 38 For as in the days before the flood, they were eating and drinking, marrying and giving in marriage, until the day Noah entered the ark, 39 and did not know until the flood came and took them all away, so will be the coming of the Son of Man. 40 Two will be in the field; one will be taken, and the other left. 41 Two women will be grinding at the mill; one will be taken, and the other left.

Matthew 24: 42 "Watch therefore, for you do not know what hour your Lord will come. 43 But know this, that if the owner of the house had known what hour the thief would come, he would have watched and not have let his house be broken into. 44 Therefore you also must be ready, for in an hour when you least expect, the Son of Man is coming.

As in the days of Noah

Jesus explained that as in the days of Noah who warned that a global flood would occur, while he built the ark; the people ignored his warning. The people did not believe his preaching and laughed at him. They continued with life as usual which was sinning. They did not believe Noah. After the ark was completely sealed and it started to rain, I'm sure there were some quick converts. They were standing in water up to their ankles and banging on the door of the ark, hoping to get in. It was too late. They had passed their chance. For 120 years Noah preached to them. They had many opportunities to get their lives right with God. They didn't want to. They wanted to live in feasts and enjoying their physical bodies and pleasures of the life. They were not concerned about God. They did not believe in God at all until the rain.

Signs in the earth

Although it has been 2000 years since Jesus words of a promise to return, it is essential that we the Church of the LORD Jesus Christ know the signs of Christ's coming. In all of the gospels, it is recorded; Jesus spoke of the signs of the season of his coming. He spoke of things that would occur; they are as signs on a road showing us that the destination is close. Although no man knows the day or hour, it is possible to know the season. Example. Right now, it is a beautiful autumn day with the light radiating through my windows. The season is Autumn. Should I take a picture of my garden, there are signs that would indicate the season. For instance, some plants and some flowers have already bloomed. Some are in full bloom. It is really pretty. It looks very different than it did a month ago. The shadows of the sun on the trees is different because the earth is revolving. It gets darker earlier than it did a month ago. In July, at 6pm, the light was pouring through the windows. Now, the sun begins to set, and the sky turns a pretty purplish pink. There are signs of the season throughout the yard.

Recent earthquakes in different places and hurricanes and storms have plagued Southern USA and the Island regions there in the Southern part of North America. Thousands of people have been displaced. Water covered landscapes, so nothing was spared. These things are sign posts. In no way would God ever send these things upon nations because the judgements of the nations is not occurring now. Surely there will be a day of the judgements of all people, but we are living in the age of the Church.

While the Holy Spirit is on the earth, there is hope for people to be saved. While we are sharing the gospel with people, some will not listen, but some will. Storms and nature's disasters occur because of the result of sin entering our world through Adam and Eve. Sin and the consequences of sin are the reason for disasters of the earth and among people. Many people are fearing the explosion of our earth from nuclear war; many people believe we will collide with other planets or meteors. Some believe that because of climate change, we will die because of the damage to the ozone layer. Although terrible things are being recorded and filmed and given to use from the media, our response should not be one of fear.

What is essential is that we Christians must remember that Jesus is coming as He promised. We should not become a part of a fallen world. We should be light in the earth pointing the way to Jesus and his soon return. My book will examine the scriptures that point to the return of the LORD. They will examine the meaning and encourage believers to obey the words of Jesus so that all people can come to know the LORD before His return.

End of Chapter questions:

1. Examine your own life to see if you are ready should the Lord come today.
2. You know that Jesus is most certainly coming anytime soon; list the priorities of your life. Give at least 5 of them.
3. List the people you would witness to should you know Jesus is coming immediately
4. List ways that you can give to the gospel – include prayer, finances, volunteering.
5. Write a letter to any unsaved loved ones explaining the rapture so that they may find it and turn to Christ should you be caught up suddenly.

2 THE ORIGIN OF SIN AND ITS AFFECTS ON THE EARTH

God created the earth and all creatures with excellence. There were no negative aspects to creation until the sin of Adam and Eve. There were no earthquakes or hurricanes or storms. It didn't even rain. A mist came up from the ground to water things. As a direct result of the sin of Adam and Eve, God pronounced judgements on man, woman, animals, the earth, the serpent and the devil. God commanded Adam and Eve to live and care for the garden; He gave them freedom in all of the trees of fruit except one: the tree of the knowledge of Good and Evil. It was the one thing God said they could not take or they would surely die.

Eve was seduced by a serpent possessed by Satan and she took of the fruit of the tree of knowledge of good and evil and gave some to Adam. They both took it. They both sinned against God. Immediately they knew they were naked. They saw things in a carnal way without the protection of God's glory that had covered them. They were fearful and ashamed. They made clothes of fig leaves to hide themselves. Please see they were only with each other, yet they felt ashamed.

The judgements or curses pronounced by God were not only on Adam and Eve but upon all people until the coming of the Messiah. As part of their sinful condition, Adam blamed Eve and Eve blamed the serpent. No one admitted they had sinned. A lack of repentance is a different kind of sin.

The origin of sin and result of sin is in the book of Genesis.

Genesis 3: 11 And He said, "Who told you that you were naked? Have you eaten from the tree of which I commanded you not to eat?"

12 The man said, "The woman whom You gave to be with me, she gave me fruit of the tree, and I ate."

13 Then the Lord God said to the woman, "What have you done?"

And the woman said, "The serpent deceived me, and I ate."

The pronouncing of judgements is on all involved and also on all of creation. The serpent is cursed; the woman would hate the serpent and there would always be fighting between the serpent (the devil and demons) and the woman (all people born on earth). Even as He utters judgements, God shows mercy towards Eve and all people by saying that the serpent would bruise his heel, but one born of women would crush its head. This is a direct prophecy related to the coming of Jesus which would occur thousands of years later.

Genesis 3: 14 The Lord God said to the serpent: "Because you have done this, You are cursed above all livestock,
    and above every beast of the field;
you will go on your belly,
    and you will eat dust
    all the days of your life.
15 I will put enmity
    between you and the woman,
    and between your offspring and her offspring;
he will bruise your head,
    and you will bruise his heel."

God's judgement on the woman was that she would now have pain in childbirth and she would desire her husband and he would rule over her. She had been created from his side; Now, she was under his authority. This situation remained until the sacrifice of the Messiah Jesus.

Genesis 3:16 To the woman He said,
"I will greatly multiply your pain in childbirth,
    and in pain you will bring forth children;
your desire will be for your husband,
    and he will rule over you."

Judgement on Adam: Judgement on the earth

God's judgement over Adam includes judgement on all the spheres of authority that Adam had been given including the earth. The earth now had thorns and thistles. Man was sentenced to hard labour. It was at this judgement, the earth was no longer protected by God's perfect condition. The earth began climate change that day. Judgement on the sin of Adam affected the earth and all the atmosphere of the earth,

Genesis 3: 17 And to Adam He said, "Because you have listened to the voice of your wife and have eaten from the tree about which I commanded you, saying, 'You shall not eat of it,'

Cursed is the ground on account of you;
   in hard labor you will eat of it
   all the days of your life.
18 Thorns and thistles it will bring forth for you,
   and you will eat the plants of the field.
19 By the sweat of your face
   you will eat bread
until you return to the ground,
   because out of it you were taken;
for you are dust,
   and to dust you will return."

The condition of the earth of course has special laws that govern in it terms of rotation and gravity and seasons etc. These things are given to us that the earth may continue to prosper, but the earth is not in its perfection. It is in a fallen state directly affected by man's sin. Jesus came as Messiah and brought peace between man and God by his death, burial and resurrection. Faith in Jesus gives us eternal hope. Also, believers in Jesus should be wise stewards of the Earth. We should care about things that affect animals, people, and natural resources. It is our responsibility to care for the earth.

Acts of nature such as earthquakes and hurricanes and tsunamis occur because the earth is in a fallen state. As Christians, we should take dominion in our areas that we live in praying for protection over our regions; we should pray for God's intervention in other regions; we should be compassionate; we should be giving; we should care for those affected by such things. Rather than blame God for disasters, we should realize the origin of all strife is sin; Only when Jesus the Messiah comes to reign on earth will there be complete peace on earth.

Even though Adam and Eve had broken covenant with God, God showed mercy on them by mentioning the hope of a deliverer who would crush the serpent's head: Messiah Jesus.

Result of the judgement over the earth affected all the earth atmosphere including the currents, winds, earth, oceans etc. Earth groans for the manifestation of sons of God in earth. Groans of the earth include the strange weather, earthquakes, etc. all creatures on the earth are part of it. All of human life is evident of it. Only when there is a new heaven and earth will all these things change,

Noah

The earth became populated by sinful people. There was hatred and killing and violence. God saw this horrible condition of the offspring of Adam and Eve in their sinful condition, but He also noticed Noah. Noah was a righteous man. He loved God. He obeyed God. God was merciful to get Noah out of His judgements of the wicked people. He also had mercy to give the people a chance to repent. Even though man was not serving God or honoring God – God gave them a chance to repent so they might enter the ark and be saved. All the earth was flooded so waters destroyed all the life outside of the ark that Noah built.

Covenant

Although the people that did not enter the Ark were drowned, Noah and his family and the animals that came to the ark were spared. The ark protected them from the world-wide flood. The water was so high that the ark finally rested on Mt. Ararat as the waters began to recede. Those who believed God were left to populate the earth. God spared the righteous and saved a remnant of people and animals to populate the earth once more.

The Noahic Covenant

God's covenant with Noah meant that He promised these things. He commanded them to replenish and populate the earth. That means he gave them dominion over the earth. God gave them the fruit of the ground. He gave them special warning about the blood of people or blood of animals. He warned them that they were never to partake of the blood of animals. He instructed them that the life of the creature is in the blood. This is a direct response to Cane in Genesis after he killed his brother. The killing of a person is sin, and God established it with Noah before He gave the commandments to Moses.

Genesis 4: 11 Now you are cursed from the ground which opened its mouth to receive your brother's blood from your hand.

It was the murdering and killing and violence that caused God to judge the earth and send rain.

Genesis 6: 11 The earth was corrupt before God and filled with violence. 12 God looked on the earth and saw it was corrupt, for all flesh had corrupted their way on the earth.

God's covenant with Noah included a promise that never again would the earth be flooded or all of the earth destroyed.

Genesis 9: 1 Then God blessed Noah and his sons and said to them, "Be fruitful and multiply and fill the earth. 2 Every beast of the earth and every bird of the sky and all that moves on the earth and all the fish of the sea will fear you and be terrified of you. They are given into your hand. 3 Every moving thing that lives will be food for you. I give you everything, just as I gave you the green plant.

4 "Only you shall not eat flesh with its life, that is, its blood. 5 But for your own lifeblood I will surely require a reckoning; from every animal will I require it; of man, too, will I require a reckoning for human life, of every man for that of his fellow man.

6 Whoever sheds the blood of man,
   by man shall his blood be shed;
for God made man
   in His own image.

7 And as for you, be fruitful and multiply; increase abundantly in the earth and multiply in it."

Don't fear the end of the earth. We have God's covenant word on it. God promised that as long as the earth would remain (which is until the new heavens and earth are created at the end of the age) there would always be seed time and harvest. That means there will always be seasons on the earth; the earth will continue to revolve around the sun; there will continue seasons on the earth. Nothing can stop it from occurring because God promised it. He cannot lie.

God's covenant promise

Genesis 8: 18 So Noah and his sons and his wife and his sons' wives went out. 19 Every beast, every creeping thing, every bird, and everything that moves on the earth, according to their families, went out of the ark.

20 Then Noah built an altar to the Lord and took of every clean animal and of every clean bird and offered burnt offerings on the altar. 21 The Lord smelled a soothing aroma; and the Lord said in His heart, "I will never again curse the ground because of man, for the inclination of man's heart is evil from his youth, nor will I again destroy every living thing as I have done.

As long as the earth remains – seed and harvest

22 While the earth remains,
seedtime and harvest,
cold and heat,
summer and winter,
and day and night
will not cease."

Conditions of the covenant

Visible sign

God gave us a visible sign of His covenant with people and animals. He placed His rainbow in the clouds after a rain so that we would see it and remember God's covenant. The rainbow is a sign of the blessing of God.

Genesis 9: 12 Then God said, "This is the sign of the covenant which I am making between Me and you and every living creature that is with you, for all future generations. 13 I have set My rainbow in the cloud, and it shall be a sign of a covenant between Me and the earth. 14 When I bring a cloud over the earth, the rainbow will be seen in the cloud; 15 then I will remember My covenant, which is between Me and you and every living creature of all flesh, and the waters will never again become a flood to destroy all flesh. 16 The rainbow will appear in the cloud, and I will see it and remember the everlasting covenant between God and every living creature of all flesh that is on the earth."

Condition of the Earth and life on the earth

The Apostle Paul talked about the condition in the earth and in all of creation as being in a groaning for an answer. The King James Version says all of creation is groaning for the manifestation of the sons of God in the earth. It literally means because of Adam's sin, all creation is in a groaning or a travail or a crying out for the solution. The solution is the manifestation of the sons of God in the earth. It means you and I. It means Christians. The earth is groaning for us to live the life of true Christians. We were given dominion over all the earth. Jesus gave his disciples authority over all the earth. It means using our faith to speak, to pray to affect all within our sphere of authority during our lives.

Matthew 28: 18 Then Jesus came and spoke to them, saying, "All authority has been given to Me in heaven and on earth. 19 Go therefore and make disciples of all nations, baptizing them in the name of the Father and of the Son and of the Holy Spirit, 20 teaching them to observe all things I have commanded you. And remember, I am with you always, even to the end of the age." Amen.

Mark 10: 19 Look, I give you authority to trample on serpents and scorpions, and over all the power of the enemy. And nothing shall by any means hurt you. 20 Nevertheless do not rejoice that the spirits are subject to you, but rather rejoice that your names are written in heaven."

Temporary

An important aspect of the groanings of the earth, for the redemption from its sinful condition is that it is temporary. Although there are situations on earth that are horrible, although there are storms, earthquakes and hurricanes, they are temporary. It is hard for humans to comprehend this because our lives on earth are also temporary. The Apostle Paul compares his sufferings to the glory of God that will be revealed in us. The glory of God is for all of eternity. Believers in Christ will live with Jesus on the present earth for 1000 years in a peaceful, joyful condition. Afterwards, Satan will be sentenced, and final judgement will come on him. There will be a new heavens and new earth. We will live forever in a world with no sin, no death, no sorrow, no evil. The longing of the true Christian is for God to bring His kingdom here on earth as it is in heaven.

Romans 8: 18 For I consider that the sufferings of this present time are not worthy to be compared with the glory which shall be revealed to us. 19 The eager expectation of the creation waits for the appearance of the sons of God. 20 For the creation was subjected to futility, not willingly, but by the will of Him who subjected it, in hope 21 that the creation itself also will be set free from its slavery to corruption into the glorious freedom of the children of God.

Groaning in the spirit

Christians who intercede for others and enter travailing prayer for others understand groanings of the Spirit. It is feeling the weight of the sinful condition and praying with all your being for God's solution. It involves pleading the blood of Jesus; it involves groaning for the kingdom to come on earth. It involves praying for the direct answer to a situation. It is comparable to child birth. It involves the pain of the curse of sin; it involves the bringing of new life, new hope (Isaiah 66).

Romans 8: 22 We know that the whole creation groans and travails in pain together until now. 23 Not only that, but we also, who have the first fruits of the Spirit, groan within ourselves while eagerly waiting for adoption, the redemption of our bodies. 24 For we are saved through hope, but hope that is seen is not hope, for why does a man still hope for what he sees? 25 But if we hope for what we do not see, we wait for it with patience.

End of chapter questions:
1. Prepare an answer (3-5 sentences) for someone who says God sent a hurricane to destroy a region of the earth.
2. Write an explanation (3-5 sentences) of why Christians should not fear the earth blowing up or being hit by other planets.
3. Explain why the rainbow is an important symbol of hope for God's people.

3 SIGNS OF JESUS COMING

Jesus not only fulfilled prophecy, He also prophesied of what would occur. The disciples were talking about the natural beauty of the rebuilt Temple at Jerusalem. It is not wrong to admire the beauty of things man creates but to focus on the beauty of something man made was not Jesus purpose in being in Jerusalem. He was directing them towards eternal things and He did it by telling them that not one stone of the temple would be left standing. Jesus knew Jerusalem would be destroyed and that Israel would be scattered. He knew that one-day Jerusalem would welcome him to come reign in the rebuilt Temple (yet to occur).

Matthew 24: 1 Jesus departed from the temple and was leaving when His disciples came to show Him the temple buildings. 2 Jesus answered them, "Do you not see all these things? Truly I say to you, not one stone shall be left here upon another that shall not be thrown down."

Matthew 23: 37 "O Jerusalem, Jerusalem, you who kill the prophets and stone those who are sent to you, how often I would have gathered your children together as a hen gathers her chicks under her wings, but you would not! 38 Look, your house is left to you desolate. 39 For I tell you, you shall not see Me again until you say, 'Blessed is He who comes in the name of the Lord.'[a]"

Jesus prophesied but also carried the weight of the prophecy as he wept over Jerusalem. He spoke words that surely would come to pass but also wept over Israel because he loved Israel and Jerusalem. God does not delight in pronouncing judgements. As He speaks words of judgements, He weeps praying the people will repent. He warns us that in the last days all nations lead by the antichrist will be attacking Israel.

Luke 21: 20 "When you see Jerusalem surrounded by armies, then you know that its desolation has drawn near. 21 Then let those who are in Judea flee to the mountains, and let those who are in the city depart, and let not those who are in the country enter it. 22 For these are the days of vengeance, that all things which are written may be fulfilled. 23 But woe to those who are pregnant and to those who nurse in those days! For there will be great distress in the land and wrath upon this people. 24 They will fall by the edge of the sword and will be led away captive to all nations. And Jerusalem will be trampled on by the Gentiles until the times of the

Gentiles are fulfilled.

The Gathering

God's judgement on Israel for wickedness – serving other gods and not honouring God was spoken through Prophets – occurred Jerusalem seized and taken over. In AD 70, it was wasted. People were killed; people were taken captive. Israel became scattered throughout the earth. They were a people without a land. Although it was prophesied that certainly it would occur, it was also prophesied that as Israel would return to God, Israel would be restored. A people without a land for thousands of years preserved their language and their heritage and in 1948 Israel was re-established. God promised to gather them again and He did. Even still there are people coming to Israel from the north, south, east and west. They are being gathered to Israel their home. God kept His covenant promise to Israel.

Ezekiel 39: 25 Therefore thus says the Lord God: Now I will restore the fortunes of Jacob and have mercy on the whole house of Israel and will be jealous for My holy name. 26 They shall forget their shame and all their trespasses by which they have trespassed against Me when they lived safely in their land and no one made them afraid. 27 When I have brought them back from the peoples and gathered them out of the lands of their enemies, then I shall be sanctified in them in the sight of many nations. 28 Then they shall know that I am the Lord their God who caused them to be led into captivity among the nations, and then gathered them again to their own land and have left none of them there anymore. 29 Nor will I hide My face from them anymore. For I will have poured out My Spirit on the house of Israel, says the Lord God.

God's judgements on Israel were because of idol worship and disobedience to the commandments. God's covenant is if they would return to Him, He would gather them.

Isaiah 11: 12 He shall set up a banner for the nations,
    and shall assemble the outcasts of Israel,
and gather together the dispersed of Judah
    from the four corners of the earth.

The restoration of Israel in 1948 is a sign of God's keeping His promised. People who were scattered all over the earth, were gathered to their original home. The regathering of Israel to her homeland, after having no land for 2000 years, is a miracle. God's faithfulness to keep His promises to Israel are an indication to us that He keeps His Word. God keeps his covenants.

God protects Israel

There are daily rocket attacks on Israel from the surrounding nations. Many cause holes in the ground; some wound people; some kill people. There are terrorist attacks that occur because of radical religious groups that hate Israel and plan to take it over, so it is no longer a country. It was noted recently in the news that the Mayor of Jerusalem encourages public citizens to defend their land by disarming and rendering helpless any terrorists. The people have boldness.

Those who hate Israel should have no place of refuge. Those who hate Israel must be disarmed. An excellent quote from the prime minister of Israel (I'm paraphrasing) is that is Israel were to stop fighting, her enemies would overtake her. If her enemies would stop fighting, there would be no more war. Israel only fights against the terrorists who hate her. It is a pretty tough way of life, but the people have a special elite guard. God Himself is the defender of Israel. He fights against those who fight against Israel. It was promised to Abraham; it was promised in all the covenants that God made with Israel.

Genesis 12: 2 I will make of you a great nation;
    I will bless you
and make your name great,
    so that you will be a blessing.
3 I will bless them who bless you
    and curse him who curses you,[a]
and in you all families of the earth
    will be blessed."

Isaiah 60: 19 The sun shall no longer be your light by day,
    nor for brightness shall the moon give light to you;
but the Lord shall be an everlasting light to you
    and your God for your glory.

If you have not seen the excellent documentary series "Against All Odds" I highly recommend it to you. In it there are examples of miraculous interventions of God to protect Israel. It quotes Bible passages such as David and Goliath, Saul and Jonathan fighting the Philistines but also discusses modern day Israel and the war in 1967. Gifts used were the gift of faith, discerning of spirits, words of wisdom and words of knowledge. God also released angels to go help Israel.

There are people who are against Israel for various reasons. There are people who align with Israel and pray for her. The truth is that God loved Israel so much out of the Apostle Paul's spirit came a prayer that all of Israel should be saved (Romans 11: 26). Also, Jesus is choosing to return to Israel. Of all places that he could choose, God chose Israel and particularly Jerusalem. Jesus will sit on the throne in the Holy of Holies in the rebuilt temple at Jerusalem. There will be 1000 years of peace and prosperity on earth during the millennial reign of Jesus. The more scriptures a Christian reads and studies, the more that person will see God's love for Israel throughout all the scriptures. God made covenant with Israel.

God will make Jerusalem a praise and a fame in the earth. God keeps Israel.

Isaiah 62: 6 I have set watchmen on your walls, O Jerusalem,
   who shall never hold their peace day nor night.
You who remind the Lord,
   do not keep silent;
7 give Him no rest until He establishes
   and makes Jerusalem a glory in the earth.

Rebuilding of the Temple Promised

The temple of Jerusalem will be rebuilt before Jesus comes to reign on earth for 1000 years. It is promised to the Prophet Daniel as a sign of the end of the age of the earth. The rebuilding of Jerusalem is promised along with the re-establishing of the daily sacrifices of animals as an offering is promised.

Daniel 9: 25 "Know therefore and understand that from the going forth of the command to restore and to rebuild Jerusalem until the Prince Messiah shall be seven weeks, and sixty-two weeks. It shall be built again, with plaza and moat, even in times of trouble. 26 After the sixty-two weeks Messiah shall be cut off and shall have nothing. And the troops of the prince who shall come shall destroy the city and the sanctuary. The end of it shall come with a flood. And until the end of the war desolations are determined. 27 And he shall make a firm covenant with many for one week. But in the middle of the week he shall cause the sacrifice and the offering to cease. And on the wing of abominations shall come one who makes desolate, until the decreed destruction is poured out on the desolator."

Daniel 12: 11 "From the time that the daily sacrifice shall be taken away and the abomination that makes desolate set up, there shall be one thousand two hundred and ninety days. 12 Blessed is he who waits and comes to the one thousand three hundred and thirty-five days.

Matthew 24: 15 "So when you see the 'abomination of desolation,'[a] spoken of by Daniel the prophet, standing in the holy place (let the reader understand), 16 then let those who are in Judea flee to the mountains.

The Rebuilding of the Temple

The sign of the rebuilding of Jerusalem and ingathering of Israel is a sign that we are drawing closer towards the end of the age as we know it. The second part has not yet come to pass and that is the rebuilding of the Temple at Jerusalem. It is promised. It does not seem to be possible right now because no one is allowed to even pray on the Temple mound. The conditions of the surrounding nations claiming ownership to it are directly against Israel rebuilding the Temple. Something will certainly change so that it could be possible. The rebuilding of the Temple is a major sign. Should you live to see the rebuilding of the Temple of Jerusalem, realize that the end of the age is certainly near. After the rebuilding of the temple, will arise an anti-Christ who will claim to be God and sit in the most Holy place of the Temple at Jerusalem. It is this point that Jesus emphasizes to his disciples. This is a sure sign of Jesus second coming.

Matthew 24: 17 Let him who is on the housetop not go down to take anything out of his house. 18 Let him who is in the field not return to take his clothes. 19 Woe to those who are with child and to those who nurse in those days! 20 Pray that your escape will not be in the winter or on the Sabbath. 21 For then will be great tribulation, such as has not happened since the beginning of the world until now, no, nor ever shall be.

Matthew 24: 22 "Unless those days were shortened, no one would be saved. But for the sake of the elect those days will be shortened. 23 Then if anyone says to you, 'Look, here is the Christ,' or 'There He is,' do not believe it. 24 For false Christs and false prophets will arise and show great signs and wonders to deceive, if possible, even the elect. 25 Listen, I have told you beforehand.

Daniel 12: 1 "And at that time Michael shall stand up, the great prince who stands guard over the sons of your people. And there shall be a time of trouble such as never was since there was a nation even to that time. And at that time your people shall be delivered, everyone who shall be found written in the book.

End of Chapter questions:
1. Explain how the nation of Israel is a sign of the coming of Jesus.
2. Give proof that God has not broken covenant with Israel.
3. Explain how fighting against Israel is a sign of Jesus Coming.

4 FALSE CHRISTS

Many people are being drawn into the supernatural into the occult and fortune tellers and astrologists and seeking to know the meaning of life. They will go on journeys to try to find the purpose of life. People will join gangs of criminals and types of secret organizations to find their place of belonging. The reason is that all creation is longing and yearning for the return of God. Their searching is a symptom of spiritual emptiness.

People will seek pleasure on earth that includes all sorts of multitasking electronic media and entertainment as a way to avoid being alone or thinking; if they keep taking in all types of stimulation of their soul, they believe they will be happy. People become drug addicts or alcoholics because they are trying to escape life. Truly without Jesus Christ, they cannot see a larger significant purpose to their lives. They may commit suicide or engage in life risking activities. Mostly the teenagers but also the 20's and 30's generations are seeking purpose for their lives. Only Jesus Christ can give them the peace they desire. Only God can fill the human spirit with His Holy Spirit bringing peace and communion with God.

False Christs and Antichrists

Some false prophets and false Christs will be able to do magic and have supernatural skills. They will appear as angels of light, but they are really deceivers who will gather people. They will use the people for selfish motives. Only by the Holy Spirit and the discerning of spirits can a Christian be spared from it.

Matthew 24: 22 "Unless those days were shortened, no one would be saved. But for the sake of the elect those days will be shortened. 23 Then if anyone says to you, 'Look, here is the Christ,' or 'There He is,' do not believe it. 24 For false Christs and false prophets will arise and show great signs and wonders to deceive, if possible, even the elect. 25 Listen, I have told you beforehand.

Wars and Persecutions

Matthew 24: 3 As He sat on the Mount of Olives, the disciples came to Him privately, saying, "Tell us, when will these things be, and what will be the sign of Your coming and of the end of the age?"

Matthew 24: 4 Jesus answered them, "Take heed that no one deceives you. 5 For many will come in My name, saying, 'I am the Christ,' and will deceive many. 6 You will hear of wars and rumors of wars. See that you are not troubled. For all these things must happen, but the end is not yet. 7 For nation will rise against nation, and kingdom against kingdom. There will be famines, epidemics, and earthquakes in various places. 8 All these are the beginning of sorrows.

What is essential here is that Jesus tells us they will arise – false prophets, false Christs. They will try to gather as many as they can into their deception. War and civil war and violence are occurring in many parts of the earth. Currently, African nations are fighting against each other; there is civil war in many of the nations. There is hatred of one tribe from another. There is religious persecution of Christians. There is slavery and murder of those not considered equal to some people because of their religion or tribe. There is civil war in many of the Arabic speaking nations such as Syria and Turkey. There is persecution of Christians and others who are hated for no reason. Many die as martyrs. Some escape. In recent years the media has filmed thousands of thousands of people trying to escape their nation in hopes for freedom and peace.

Luke 21: 12 "But before all these things, they will seize you and persecute you, delivering you up to the synagogues and prisons, and you will be brought before kings and governors for My name's sake. 13 It will turn out as a testimony for you. 14 Therefore resolve in your hearts beforehand not to practice your defense. 15 For I will give you a mouth and wisdom, which all your opponents will be able to neither refute nor resist. 16 You will be betrayed by parents and brothers and relatives and friends. And they will put some of you to death. 17 You will be hated by all men for My name's sake, 18 but not a hair of your head shall perish. 19 In your endurance you will gain your souls.

Jesus prophesied about persecution of believers

Jesus prophesied to the disciples that people would hate them because they were followers of Jesus. Although it was fulfilled by all of the Apostles, I also believe it is a word that applies to us today. Although we in North America and in Western Society enjoy religious freedom to worship God, there are countries where Christians are persecuted and abused and made as slaves because of their faith.

John 15: 18 "If the world hates you, you know that it hated Me before it hated you. 19 If you were of the world, the world would love you as its own. But because you are not of the world, since I chose you out of the world, the world therefore hates you. 20 Remember the word that I said to you: 'A servant is not greater than his master.' If they persecuted Me, they will also persecute you. If they kept My words, they will keep yours also. 21 But all these things they will do to you for My name's sake, because they do not know Him who sent Me. 22 If I had not come and spoken to them, they would not have had sin. But now they have no excuse for their sin. 23 He who hates Me hates My Father also. 24 If I had not performed among them the works which no one else did, they would have no sin. But now have they seen and hated both My Father and Me. 25 But that the word which is written in their law might be fulfilled, 'They hated Me without a cause.'[a]

Jesus prophesied to strengthen believers

Jesus told them of things to come so they would receive the comfort of his words. They would know Jesus was with them and that they should not fear.

John 16: 1 "I have spoken these things to you so that you will not fall away. 2 They will put you out of the synagogues. Yes, the time is coming that whoever kills you will think that he is offering a service to God. 3 They will do these things to you, because they have not known the Father, nor Me. 4 I have told you these things, so that when the time comes, you may remember that I told you about them.

These are symptoms of the groaning of the earth people's groups. People yearn for freedom. People do not want to obey despots or dictators. Many governmental systems in our earth are unjust and without care for the people of their nation. We in North America and in Europe and Australia enjoy freedom many people long for. They are coming from all nations trying to find refuge from their unjust rulers. There are famines especially in Africa but other places as well where the people are starving because there are no crops because of no rain. Ethiopia and Sudan are especially in drought and famine, so the United Nations appealed for financial and other aide for these countries. These are symptoms of the groaning or travail of creation. It affects thousands and thousands of people.

In some nations it is illegal to be a Christian, so many people quietly worship and serve God rather than die. Some people will betray secret Christians for a price. They may turn on their own family members either killing them or turning them over to a government that will deal unjustly with them. Certainly, there is hatred of other groups as well but there is a hatred of Christians in some nations because of the freedom, peace and abundant life that it promises to believers. Those who realize that God wants to prosper them and bless them will yearn for full freedom. They will not be content with less than God's best for them. There are countries that Christians are martyred for their faith such as China, Iran, Iraq, North Korea, Nigeria, Sudan etc.

Resist those with evil agendas

It is my prayer and my hope that the Western World (North America and Europe and all the British Commonwealth nations) will always remain free; we must remember what occurred in Nazi Germany. We should remember that people can work together for good to accomplish mighty wonderful things in the earth; if we join together in alliance for peace and freedom, we can do much good. People could also be deceived by powerful leaders who lie to them and cause them to believe that some people are less than human. Prejudice or hatred of any people should not be tolerated by the United Nations or any democratic people. Countries that exist to fight other countries and nations with a goal of taking over the whole world must be noted and the global alliances for peace and freedom must resist and as necessary fight against these nations.

If you deny Christ - Repent

They will abuse and use and hate people believing they are correct. If we allow these people to have any power of authority, they will affect the generations we live in and the generations to come. We would lose the freedoms that we so dearly cherish in our democratic society. If something should occur so that you are threatened on your life to denounce Christ, if you should weaken and outwardly deny Christ before your accusers, please know God will forgive you if you repent. Peter denied Jesus 3 X. Peter feared for his life. He repented, and Jesus forgave Him. The Christians in the early church knew this type of persecution and many died as martyrs. Some denied Christ and served him secretly. Please repent and know God forgives you.

Luke 22: 54 Then they arrested Him, and led Him away, and brought Him into the high priest's house. Peter followed at a distance. 55 But when they had kindled a fire in the middle of the courtyard and sat down together, Peter sat among them. 56 Then a servant girl saw him as he sat near the fire, and gazed at him, and said, "This man was with Him."

Luke 22: 57 But he denied Him, saying, "Woman, I do not know Him."

Luke 22: 58 A little later someone else saw him and said, "You also are one of them."

Peter said, "Man, I am not!"

Luke 22: 59 About an hour later another man firmly declared, "Certainly, this man also was with Him, for he is a Galilean."

Luke 22: 60 Peter said, "Man, I do not know what you are saying." Immediately, while he was yet speaking, the rooster crowed. 61 The Lord turned and looked at Peter. Then Peter remembered the word of the Lord, how He had told him, "Before the rooster crows, you will deny Me three times." 62 And Peter went outside and wept bitterly.

The passage below speaks of iniquity and loss of love. Because people are bombarded with some much negative news, they become hardened. They develop a thick skin or a harsh attitude about things. They become non-caring. People may witness a crime or violence and not do anything because of their hardened hearts. As in the days of Noah, not only was there feasting and seeking pleasure, but also violence covered all the earth. The sin of Cane was rampant throughout the earth with murders and other kinds of violence.

Sinful condition on the earth

Before Jesus returns, the sinful condition of the earth is going to be as darkness. People will be violent; people will be self centred with qualities that are sinful as mentioned in the scriptures. These ungodly fleshly characteristics describe someone living in the last days who does not know Christ.

2 Timothy 3: 3 Know this: In the last days perilous times will come. 2 Men will be lovers of themselves, lovers of money, boastful, proud, blasphemers, disobedient to parents, unthankful, unholy, 3 without natural affection, trucebreakers, slanderers, unrestrained, fierce, despisers of those who are good, 4 traitors, reckless, conceited, lovers of pleasures more than lovers of God, 5 having a form of godliness, but denying its power. Turn away from such people.

Although it is true, and we should note these things, we should realize that as long as we are on earth there is hope for all people to be saved. Because the Holy Spirit lives on the inside of us, we can share the gospel with people who are sinful, and they can be changed. They can be born again as we once were. All of us were born in sin. It is only through Jesus blood that we are forgiven; we are made holy; we are the righteousness of God in Jesus Christ (2 Corinthians 5: 21). We should share Christ with as many people as we can, so they too may come to know God.

Light of the Church in the world

Jesus calls believers light in the world. We who have experienced unconditional love of God through Jesus Christ can love others with the same love. A person who has never known the compassion of a Saviour cannot possibly love in the same way (1 John 4: 19). It is God's love in us that compels us to share Christ with others. In this way, we are as lights bringing the love of God to people who never knew God.

Matthew 5: 14 "You are the light of the world. A city that is set on a hill cannot be hidden. 15 Neither do men light a candle and put it under a basket, but on a candlestick. And it gives light to all who are in the house. 16 Let your light so shine before men that they may see your good works and glorify your Father who is in heaven.

Isaiah received a prophetic word about the situation. The light of God will radiate on and through His people shining brightly amidst the darkness of the earth. The way to fight the darkness is to shine the light of God's love, God's mercy, God's compassion and by doing it in practical ways such as giving financially, caring for the poor, those who need healing, those who are oppressed. We will stand out clearly as standards of God's love just as torches light the sky at night.

Isaiah 60: Arise, shine, for your light has come,
    and the glory of the Lord has risen upon you.
2 For the darkness shall cover the earth
    and deep darkness the peoples;
but the Lord shall rise upon you,
    and His glory shall be seen upon you.
3 The nations shall come to your light
    and kings to the brightness of your rising.

Although there is surely going to be darkness, the Church will shine brightly the glory of God. God has promised to send His Spirit upon all people groups on the earth. What that means is global revival such as we have never known. People will be saved. People will be baptized with the Holy Spirit. People all over the earth will know that Jesus is Lord. All people will have opportunity to know God. Part of the signs of the second coming include Joel's description of the revival to come.

Joel 2: 28 And it will be that, afterwards,
    I will pour out My Spirit on all flesh;
then your sons and your daughters will prophesy,
    your old men will dream dreams,
    and your young men will see visions.
29 Even on the menservants and maidservants
    in those days I will pour out My Spirit.
30 Then I will work wonders in the heavens
    and the earth—
    blood and fire and columns of smoke.
31 The sun will be turned to darkness,
    and the moon to blood,
    before the great and awe-inspiring day of the Lord comes.
32 And it will be that everyone
    who calls on the name of the Lord will be saved.
For on Mount Zion and in Jerusalem
    there will be deliverance,
    as the Lord has said,
and among the survivors
    whom the Lord calls.

Jesus Parable about the net

Most certainly the righteous will be separated from the unrighteous. Only God can do it.

Matthew 13: 47 "Again, the kingdom of heaven is like a net that was cast into the sea and gathered all kinds of fish. 48 When it was full, they drew it to shore, sat down, and gathered the good into baskets, but threw the bad away. 49 So shall it be at the end of the world. The angels will come out and separate the evil from the righteous 50 and throw them into the fiery furnace. There will be wailing and gnashing of teeth."

There is a scene around the throne of God shown in Revelation. There is such a multitude of people who are redeemed, it is too large to number. That may not seem like much except the group that were saved out of the tribulation period are numbered and there are 144 thousand of them. A multitude too large to number would have to exceed that number by much. We should be preaching and teaching Christ to all nations; multitudes shall be saved, healed and delivered. It isn't reasonable that God would only let some be saved. Surely God will save all those who call on him in truth. All people should be given the chance to accept Christ.

Revelation 7: 9 Then I looked. And there was a great multitude which no one could count, from all nations and tribes and peoples and tongues, standing before the throne and before the Lamb, clothed with white robes, with palm branches in their hands. 10 They cried out with a loud voice:

"Salvation belongs to our God
who sits on the throne,
and to the Lamb!"

Global revival

Israel will be grafted once more into the tree – Israel will come to know Jesus as Messiah. Although Israel did not receive Jesus as Messiah in his first coming, they will certainly receive him in his next coming. The Apostle Paul shares this with the Christians. We Christians are "grafted' or welcomed into the tree of Abraham through faith in Jesus Christ. God's mercy is still towards those "branches" of Israel that did not receive him as Messiah. It is God's desire that all of Israel would come to know him.

Romans 11: 17 But if some of the branches were broken off, and you, being a wild olive shoot, were grafted in among them and became a partaker with them of the root and richness of the olive tree, 18 do not boast against the branches. If you boast, remember you do not sustain the root, but the root sustains you. 19 You will say then, "The branches were broken off, so that I might be grafted in." 20 This is correct. They were broken off because of unbelief, but you stand by faith. Do not be arrogant, but fear. 21 For if God did not spare the natural branches, neither will He spare you.

Romans 11: 22 Therefore consider the goodness and severity of God— severity toward those who fell, but goodness toward you, if you continue in His goodness. Otherwise, you also will be cut off. 23 And these also, if they do not remain in unbelief, will be grafted in, for God is able to graft them in again. 24 For if you were cut out of the olive tree which is wild by nature, and were grafted contrary to nature into a cultivated olive tree, how much more will these, who are the natural branches, be grafted into their own olive tree?

The Apostle Paul prophesies over Israel as he teaches about Israel's accepting of Jesus as Messiah. Jews and Gentiles will worship God together.

Romans 11: 25 For I do not want you to be ignorant of this mystery, brothers, lest you be wise in your own estimation, for a partial hardening has come upon Israel until the fullness of the Gentiles has come in. 26 And so all Israel will be saved, as it is written:

"The Deliverer will come out of Zion,
    and He will remove ungodliness from Jacob";[e]
27 "for this is My covenant with them,
    when I shall take away their sins."[f]

It is God's heart that all of Israel, all of the Christians be made as one in Messiah. God in his mercy towards us, Christians is no less than His mercy towards Israel. God's heart is for all people to know Him. Jesus Christ is the Messiah; Jesus Christ is the Saviour; Jesus Christ is LORD. Revelation of Jesus as Messiah will come to the Jewish believers.

Zechariah 12: 10 And I will pour out on the house of David and over those dwelling in Jerusalem a spirit of favor and supplication so that they look to Me, whom they have pierced through. And they will mourn over him as one mourns for an only child and weep bitterly over him as a firstborn. 11 On that day the mourning in Jerusalem will be as great as that of Hadad Rimmon in the plain of Megiddo.

John 19: 36 For these things happened so that the Scripture should be fulfilled, "Not one of His bones shall be broken,"[b] 37 and again another Scripture says, "They shall look on Him whom they have pierced."[c]

Revelation 1: 7 Look! He is coming with clouds,
    and every eye will see Him,
even those who pierced Him.

And all the tribes of the earth will mourn because of Him.
Even so, Amen.

World Revival: The Gospel Preached

Because Jesus commanded us to preach the gospel to all creatures until his return, we should be doing it. The Church is doing it. There are satellites that broadcast Christian programming throughout the earth. Technology is such that TV and Cables and Satellite and Internet have made it possible to reach every people group in cities or towns. There are missionary organizations that send relief to feed, clothe and teach life skills to people in poverty. They also teach the scriptures. Some Bible printing and distributing organizations also give digital audio Bibles to those who only use oral communication. Literacy skills are taught including the Bible as reading material. The Bible is currently, constantly being translated into the languages of all different types of people groups. Social Media makes it easy to spread the gospel quickly and efficiently at almost no cost. Blog posts make it possible to preach the gospel and have it saved so people researching information can find facts about almost any topic. Even in countries where the people cannot openly worship God, the gospel is obtainable through digital media. The gospel is being preached.

Even yet, there are unreached people groups. There are cities with millions of people in them where Christianity is outlawed, and no one has had opportunity to receive Christ. There are countries that persecute Christians, so all Christians do not have a Bible unless it is smuggled into the country. Although we are reaching people, we must continue to target all people groups so that the commission may be completed.

Matthew 24: 14 And this gospel of the kingdom will be preached throughout the world as a testimony to all nations, and then the end will come.

It is essential that Christians design creative ways of bringing the gospel to all different types of people. It is essential that our message is pure and not given for selfish gain. The simple truths of scripture must be presented in all types of media such as print, digital, audio; movies and documentaries, dramas, musicals and creative writing. Different types of study Bibles and helps must be made available to people who live very differently than we do in North America. We must do all that we can to continue preaching the gospel.

God's Word

God's word must be made available to all people. I would advocate a Bible channel on both audio and video satellite so that God's word can be received any time by any one. There is going to be an ingathering of souls into the kingdom of God or global harvest beyond what we have ever known.

Matthew 22: 8 "Then he said to his servants, 'The wedding is ready, but those who were invited were not worthy. 9 Go therefore to the streets, and invite to the wedding banquet as many as you find.' 10 So those servants went out into the streets and gathered together as many as they found, both bad and good. So the wedding hall was filled with guests.

John 4: 35 Do you not say, 'There are yet four months, and then comes the harvest'? Listen! I say to you, lift up your eyes and look at the fields, for they are already white for harvest. 36 He who reaps receives wages, and gathers fruit that leads to eternal life, that both he who sows and he who reaps may rejoice together. 37 For in this is the saying true, 'One sows, and another reaps.' 38 I sent you to reap a crop for which you did not labor. And you have benefited from their labor."

Jesus was telling the disciples to lift their eyes to see that the earth is the harvest field and they should be preaching and teaching. The same message is true today. God promises that God's place of worship will be raised up in the last days and people will know where to go to find God's word. People will willingly come to learn of God. Their hearts will be softened. There will be desire of people to know the ways of God.

Isiah 2: 2 In the last days,
the mountain of the Lord's house shall be established
    on the top of the mountains,
and shall be exalted above the hills,
    and all nations shall flow to it.

3 Many people shall go and say,
"Come, and let us go up to the mountain of the Lord,
    to the house of the God of Jacob,
and He will teach us of His ways,
    and we will walk in His paths."
For out of Zion shall go forth the law,
    and the word of the Lord from Jerusalem.
4 He shall judge among the nations,
    and shall rebuke many peoples;
and they shall beat their swords into plowshares,
    and their spears into pruning hooks;
nation shall not lift up sword against nation,
    nor shall they learn war any more.

5 O house of Jacob, come,
    and let us walk in the light of the Lord.

Our churches should be places that feed the Christians and equip them for ministry. We should all be pursuing evangelism in some way. The presence of God in a church will produce the miraculous: salvation, healing, deliverance. There will be signs and wonders following us, and people will know where to go to get a healing or a miracle. We will be God's people of faith who live what we believe so that God can use us to pray, to heal, to cast our demons etc.

The way the Church is to be as a light in the world is that we are different. We have the manifest presence of God in our midst like Israel had the Ark of the covenant with the presence of God. We are the carriers of God's Holy Spirit or His glory on the earth. We must be the people to attract those who want to know God.

End of Chapter questions:
1. Give evidence that God knows about false prophets and false Christs.
2. List reason a Christian should not be fearful of false prophets or false Christs.
3. Explain how there will be a harvest of souls or revival before Christ's coming.

5 CONDITIONS FOR THE RAPTURE

Matthew 24: 9 "Then they will hand you over to be persecuted and will kill you. And you will be hated by all nations for My name's sake. 10 Then many will fall away, and betray one another, and hate one another. 11 And many false prophets will rise and will deceive many. 12 Because iniquity will abound, the love of many will grow cold. 13 But he who endures to the end shall be saved. 14 And this gospel of the kingdom will be preached throughout the world as a testimony to all nations, and then the end will come.

Any of us who studied the events of World War I and World War II are overwhelmed by the way that people blindly followed orders to kills people and treat people in horrible ways. The allied forces who gave their lives to keep the world free sacrificed everything so that we could keep our democracy. The only difference between those years and these years is that nuclear weapons are rampant not only among our allies but also among our enemies. People that hate us – who hate democracy and freedom as we know it have nuclear weapons. Truly nuclear war would affect millions of people and cause the earth we know to be forever damaged perhaps permanently.

The Rise of the Antichrist

During World War I and World War II there was global war with losses of life and destruction beyond any previous historical war. There will arise hatred towards the Jews – attack of the nations that hate her. The Old Testament and the New Testament warn us that there will arise an Antichrist a person in leadership – who will affect all the nations and promise global peace. For that to arise, there must be war and destruction. The wars and destruction of people and places on earth are a sign.

The Antichrist will promise world peace. He will not only speak it, he will be in a position of authority with such respect and reverence because of his deceptive appearance as a Saviour of the people that people will yield themselves to him. He will be a global leader who will promise world peace and have the ability to do it. For 3 ½ years people will enjoy the false peace the antichrist brings. They will believe that he may be the Messiah. During global peace, we may have opportunity to preach Christ to more nations. Antichrist will go in the rebuilt Temple and declare himself God – abomination because he is possessed by Satan.

Global War

Luke 21: 10 Then He said to them, "Nation will rise against nation, and kingdom against kingdom. 11 Great earthquakes will occur in various places, and there will be famines and pestilence. And there will be terrors and great signs from heaven.

Jesus gives us warning about the Antichrist. There have been many who have deceived people by believing they are the Christ. People were deceived by lying signs and wonders. There are people on earth presently who are worshipped as god by some people. One will fulfill the prophecy warning that there would come terrible things on the earth The Antichrist will be given global power by appearing to be a solution to war. His ideas will charm the nations. He will ascend to a place of global significance. He will bring peace, but then he will turn on the people and horrible things will be done.

The period that follows The Antichrist's rule over the people is known as the tribulation period. It includes the horrible acts of the Antichrist but also God's judgements on the nations. There is teaching of the Rapture or catching up of the Church into heaven to protect and preserve the Church. The beliefs vary. I give you a brief summary of the beliefs concerning the rapture. There are books on each of these theories should you want more information. I only mention them briefly so that you may know that among believers there is difference of interpretation although all 3 believe in the rapture.

Theories of when it will occur differ. I have not recently heard strong teaching of the rapture, so I give you the three beliefs that you may research them further.

Jesus Promise to Protect the Elect

Revelation 3: 10 Because you have kept My word of patience, I also will keep you from the hour of temptation which shall come upon the entire world, to test those who dwell on the earth.

Pre tribulation- I am a member of this group of believers who believe that the Rapture will occur before the tribulation because God saved Lots family even though all of Sodom and Gomorrah were destroyed. He sent angels to deliver them out of their place. God preserved Noah and his family and some of each of the animal species so that there was a remnant of believers saved. God does not punish the innocent with the guilty. These are primary reasons I interpret the scriptures to mean that we can escape the tribulation by the rapture of the Church.

Mid tribulationist- This group of believers interpret the scriptures to believe that for 3 ½ years of the Antichrist's reign, the church will remain on the earth in the tribulation under the antichrist. They believe they will be evangelizing while the antichrist is hunting and killing Christians in severe persecution. They interpret the scripture to mean that Jesus will spare them from the most severe part of the tribulation.

Post tribulationist- There are many reputable ministries and churches that believe that the Church will live on earth as a witness for God all throughout the judgements on the earth and through the persecution of the Antichrist. They believe that God will sovereignly protect and spare some people from death, so they can share Christ. They believe the rapture of the Church will occur once Jesus comes to rule and reign in Jerusalem on the throne in Jerusalem's rebuilt temple.

The Abomination

Abomination means utterly disgusting to God – sacrilege. The Antichrist will proclaim himself as Messiah, King and Lord in the rebuilt temple at Jerusalem. It is the place that later King Jesus will come to and reign from for 1000 years. It is an abomination at a person would proclaim himself or herself to be God. The Antichrist will be possessed by Satan so that he can appear as an angel of light or a true good person. He will be able to do many signs and wonders. He will point to himself as god. He will draw many people into his deception because of his ability to do lying signs and wonders – they are magic rather than true miracles.

The Antichrist will seem to die but seem to be resurrected in a mockery of Jesus. Many people will be deceived believing it is true because of his temporary peace that the antichrist brings. Jesus warns us that if we are to see a person proclaim himself as God, it is one of the last signs of Jesus second coming. He tells people to flee their places – to get away. When the true Messiah Jesus comes, all people of the earth will see Him and know who He is. The Antichrist uses trickery and lies to gather people. Those 3 ½ years of peace he promises will be followed by 3 ½ years of horror upon earth such as the whole world has never experienced. Part of the horror is things the Antichrist will do; there will be persecution of believers. He will turn on the people and incite war. He will hate Israel and try to destroy her. Part is the judgements of God that will come on the nations after the rapture.

Matthew 24: 15 "So when you see the 'abomination of desolation,'[a] spoken of by Daniel the prophet, standing in the holy place (let the reader understand), 16 then let those who are in Judea flee to the mountains. 17 Let him who is on the housetop not go down to take anything out of his house. 18 Let him who is in the field not return to take his clothes. 19 Woe to those who are with child and to those who nurse in those days! 20 Pray that your escape will not be in the winter or on the Sabbath. 21 For then will be great tribulation, such as has not happened since the beginning of the world until now, no, nor ever shall be.

Signs of the Rapture

Even in this horrible period, God shortens the days, so the elect can be saved. God shows mercy towards the elect or the people of God that are left as a remnant on the earth. Christians should not follow someone who claims to be Messiah. When Jesus comes – He will descend visibly from the heaven on the Mt. of Olives. Jesus appearing will be a global occurrence. All people will know it is Jesus. They will see the scars in his feet and his hands. They will recognize Him, but it will be too late for them to turn to Christ. As Jesus appears, the Church on the earth will be caught up to be with Jesus to escape the judgements and horror that will be on the earth.

Matthew 24: 22 "Unless those days were shortened, no one would be saved. But for the sake of the elect those days will be shortened. 23 Then if anyone says to you, 'Look, here is the Christ,' or 'There He is,' do not believe it. 24 For false Christs and false prophets will arise and show great signs and wonders to deceive, if possible, even the elect. 25 Listen, I have told you beforehand. If any person or media or type of communication announces in human ways of communicating that Christ has returned to the earth – know it is a lie. If you are a Christian, you will see Jesus return. You will not wonder about it; you will know that it is Christ. All will see Him throughout all of the earth.

Matthew 24: 26 "So, if they say to you, 'Look, He is in the desert,' do not go there; or, 'Look, He is in the private chambers,' do not believe it. 27 For as the lightning comes from the east and flashes to the west, so will be the coming of the Son of Man. 28 Wherever the carcass is, there the eagles will be gathered together.

The Coming of Christ: The Rapture of the Church

Signs in the earth and planets and heavenly realm

Unusual planet activity will occur. Strange things in the realms of the heavens will occur as a sign of things be changed in the realms of the earth.

Joel 2: 30 Then I will work wonders in the heavens
and the earth—
blood and fire and columns of smoke.
31 The sun will be turned to darkness,
and the moon to blood,
before the great and awe-inspiring day of the Lord comes.

The sign of Jesus - rapture
Matthew 24: 29 "Immediately after the tribulation of those days,

'the sun will be darkened,
the moon will not give its light;
the stars will fall from heaven,
and the powers of the heavens will be shaken.'[b]

The Coming of the Son of Man

Many people will be fearful of the strange occurrences in the heavens and the weather abnormalities on the earth. All of creation is going to be shaken because of the things that will come upon the earth.

Luke 21: 25 "There will be signs in the sun and the moon and the stars; and on the earth distress of nations, with perplexity, the sea and the waves roaring; 26 men fainting from fear and expectation of what is coming on the inhabited earth. For the powers of heaven will be shaken. 27 Then they will see the Son of Man coming in a cloud with power and great glory. 28 When these things begin to happen, look up and lift up your heads, for your redemption is drawing near."

Luke 21: 26 "Then they will see the Son of Man coming in clouds with great power and glory. 27 Then He will send His angels and gather His elect from the four winds, from the farthest part of the earth to the farthest part of heaven.

Jesus will appear so that all nations will see him. He will come in glory as King of Kings and Lord of Lords. His angels will gather the elect of God from all of the earth. We who are believers will literally be caught up into the air to be with Jesus. There is an excellent series of books by Tim Hahaye about the rapture and life on earth after it. If you have not seen the Left Behind Series of movies or read the books, I highly recommend them. They show what could occur.

The Rapture

As we are caught up to be with Jesus we will be immediately caught up. If we are driving or flying or using transportation, all those vehicles will be left suddenly. Most certainly there will crashes and strange occurrences with millions of Christians suddenly missing. Those who we shared Christ with may remember at that moment of seeing Jesus, but if they did not repent and accept Jesus, they will be left behind. There will be multitudes who are affected by vanishing.

It is essential that we share the truth of the rapture to the people around us so that if they should see Jesus and suddenly all of the Christian go missing, they will know they should give their lives to God immediately. It is too late for them to ascend in the rapture, but it is not too late for them to be saved, God can forgive them, strengthen them and give them wisdom beyond the wisdom of the earth or of the Antichrist. There will be many who are converts after the Rapture. They will live through the tribulation period. There will be horrors on the earth both from the antichrist and from the judgements of the nations. The study of the tribulation is a topic of its own. It is covered in the book of Revelation but also in the Old Testament in Daniel and Ezekiel.

Matthew 24: 30 "Then the sign of the Son of Man will appear in heaven, and then all the tribes of the earth will mourn, and they will see the Son of Man coming on the clouds of heaven with power and great glory. 31 And He will send His angels with a great sound of a trumpet, and they shall gather His elect from the four winds, from one end of the heavens to the other.

Know the season by the fruit

Know the season by the fig tree example – know the season of these things occurring as proof that Jesus word is coming to pass. Jesus promised surely these things would occur. He wasn't stating what he thought or what he desired. He was telling what certainly occur – prophetic word. Jesus makes it so clear that all of these things must come to pass before His return. They are signs. The signs point the way to what certainly occur. For instance, signs announcing a restaurant appear on the highway before the exit for the restaurant. As surely as you can tell the season of a plant or tree, by its leaves and fruit, you can know the sign of the coming of Jesus.

The Lesson of the Fig Tree

Matthew 24: 32 "Now learn this lesson from the fig tree: When its branch becomes tender and grows leaves, you know that summer is near. 33 So also, when you shall see all these things, you know that it is near, even at the doors. 34 Truly I say to you, this generation will not pass away until all these things take place. 35 Heaven and earth will pass away, but My words will never pass away.

The Unknown Day and Hour

Never believe someone found a way to figure out the day. Do not be deceived. Throughout my life there have been several North American religions and denominations and preachers who believed the end was coming and that God gave them the exact day. They announced the day to the media and the media filmed them and all people expected, and some were fearful. They were deceived. At the least – those predicting a day of Jesus return, will appear embarrassed and lose the people following them. Yes, all of them had many people believing the lie. The power to persuade people is multiplied by conviction. I truly believe those leaders were deceived and not just trying to fool people. Nevertheless, they are guilty of contradicting the scriptures that clearly tell us that no man knows the day or the hour. If Jesus spoke these words, we must believe them no matter how much we believe we are the exception to the scriptures. It is a sin to contradict scripture. If those people will repent, God will forgive them.

During the last 50 years there have been lying antichrists and those who predicted the end of the world. Currently there are people living in religious cults – deceived believing a person is the Messiah. There are some countries where a person claims to be God and the people follow him and worship him as though he is God. We are not to fear them, we are not to socialize with them; should we be given a chance, we should witness the truth of Jesus to them.

As suddenly as the rain drops occurred after Noah and his family and the animals were inside the ark, so shall the rapture of the Church occur. One will be taken or caught up in the rapture; the other will be left behind. The selection is if they believed in Jesus Christ as Saviour or not.

Matthew 24: 36 "Concerning that day and hour no one knows, not even the angels of heaven, but My Father only. 37 As were the days of Noah, so will be the coming of the Son of Man. 38 For as in the days before the flood, they were eating and drinking, marrying and giving in marriage, until the day Noah entered the ark, 39 and did not know until the flood came and took them all away, so will be the coming of the Son of Man. 40 Two will be in the field; one will be taken, and the other left. 41 Two women will be grinding at the mill; one will be taken, and the other left.

Always be ready

Jesus warns us to "watch". I believe He literally means to notice the signs of His coming being aware that the end is near. I also believe He means that we should be careful. We should live our lives wholly unto God with no unconfessed sins or iniquities. Watch meaning – be careful. He also says that even though we note the signs and the season, it will still come suddenly. We won't be expecting it. Watch - in itself is a warning. As in the 'semper paratis' always be ready, we as Christians should live ready to go but living our lives giving and serving and living all aspects of our human life as a witness for God. We should live each day fully giving God glory in all aspects of our lives. We must also care for people and share Christ with them, knowing the end of the age is near.

Matthew 24: 42 "Watch therefore, for you do not know what hour your Lord will come. 43 But know this, that if the owner of the house had known what hour the thief would come, he would have watched and not have let his house be broken into. 44 Therefore you also must be ready, for in an hour when you least expect, the Son of Man is coming.

During the Rapture

In less than a moment, we who are expecting Jesus Christ's return will be transformed. Our physical body will be changed so that we will ascend up to God. We will be caught up to be with God. We will remain ourselves but with a new body – a spiritual body. We will not die. We will be changed. It is a hope for all Christians. Jesus is coming as He promised he would. We who are in Christ will be raptured or caught up.

1 Corinthians 15: 51 Listen, I tell you a mystery: We shall not all sleep, but we shall all be changed. 52 In a moment, in the twinkling of an eye, at the last trumpet, for the trumpet will sound, the dead will be raised incorruptible, and we shall be changed. 53 For this corruptible will put on incorruption, and this mortal will put on immortality. 54 When this

corruptible will have put on incorruption, and this mortal will have put on immortality, then the saying that is written shall come to pass: "Death is swallowed up in victory."[d]

The New Body: The Resurrected Body

1 Corinthians15: 35 But someone will say, "How are the dead raised up? With what body do they come?" 36 You fool! What you sow is not made alive unless it dies. 37 When you sow, you do not sow the body that shall be, but a bare kernel, perhaps of wheat or of some other grain. 38 Then God gives it a body as He pleases, and to each seed its own body. 39 All flesh is not the same flesh. There is one kind of flesh of men, another flesh of beasts, another of fish, and another of birds. 40 There are also celestial bodies and terrestrial bodies. The glory of the celestial is one, and the glory of the terrestrial is another. 41 There is one glory of the sun, and another glory of the moon, and another glory of the stars. One star differs from another star in glory.

42 So also is the resurrection of the dead. The body is sown in corruption; it is raised in incorruption. 43 It is sown in dishonor, it is raised in glory. It is sown in weakness, it is raised in power. 44 It is sown a natural body, it is raised a spiritual body.

There is a natural body, and there is a spiritual body. 45 So it is written, "The first man Adam was made a living soul."[c] The last Adam was made a life-giving spirit. 46 However, that which is spiritual is not first, but the natural, and then the spiritual. 47 The first man was of the earth, made of dust; the second man was the Lord from heaven. 48 As was the man of dust, so are those who are of dust; and as is the man of heaven, so are those who are of heaven. 49 As we have borne the image of the man of dust, we shall also bear the image of the man of heaven.

50 Now this I say, brothers, that flesh and blood cannot inherit the kingdom of God, nor does corruption inherit incorruption. 51 Listen, I tell you a mystery: We shall not all sleep, but we shall all be changed. 52 In a moment, in the twinkling of an eye, at the last trumpet, for the trumpet will sound, the dead will be raised incorruptible, and we shall be changed. 53 For this corruptible will put on incorruption, and this mortal will put on immortality. 54 When this corruptible will have put on incorruption, and this mortal will have put on immortality, then the saying that is written shall come to pass: "Death is swallowed up in victory."[d]

55 "O death, where is your sting?

O grave, where is your victory?"[e]

56 The sting of death is sin, and the strength of sin is the law. 57 But thanks be to God, who gives us the victory through our Lord Jesus Christ!

Phil 3: 20 But our citizenship is in heaven, from where also we await for our Savior, the Lord Jesus Christ, 21 who will transform our body of humiliation, so that it may be conformed to His glorious body, according to the working of His power even to subdue all things to Himself.

All people of the earth will see Jesus, but many will weep because they did not believe, and they will be left behind. It will be too late for them to be caught up with the Church in the rapture, but they can still repent and turn to Christ although they will be living on earth through the most horrible part of earth's existence.

End of Chapter Questions:

1. Define and explain the rapture of the Church.
2. Research the Pretribulationist, Mid tribulationsist view and the post tribulationist views and pray about it. Prepare your heart to live with what you believe.
3. Jesus is coming to rapture or catch up his church. Explain how we will know it is the true Christ rather than a false Christ.

6 CHRISTIAN LIFE

It matters what we are doing. God those who are faithful will be honoring God always. Christians should be living each day as though fully for God. We should daily give our whole self to God: spirit, soul and body. It Involves all areas of life. Holiness is not often talked about in the Christian media at present. Living with the word of God as the standard for life is the only way we can live Holy. We must know the scriptures; we must keep the scriptures. We must keep God's word as the priority for all decisions. Keeping God's words in our eyes, in our ears and in our mouths, will help it to get down into our hearts. Literally the engrafted word can save our souls (James 1: 21).

1 Thessalonians 5: 23 May the very God of peace sanctify you completely. And I pray to God that your whole spirit, soul, and body be preserved blameless unto the coming of our Lord Jesus Christ. 24 Faithful is He who calls you, who also will do it.

Believers will be judged on what we did with Jesus. Knowing about God isn't enough. We are to share Christ with all people: The Great Commission. Christians should be living each day to the fullest. The disciples were commanded to preach the gospel to every creature, in all nations. I believe it literally. In each place we are in our schools, work places, homes, society, we should be sharing the truth about Jesus Christ with people.

We should care for people enough to tell them. Some people will accept Christ. To others, it is a seed. Try to speak some scripture to the person and pray over it. The scripture will be quickened in the person and bring forth fruit. Preaching is not just for pastors and apostles, prophets, evangelists and teachers in the ministry. It is a commandment to all Christians. We should be sharing Christ. We should be baptizing people – either literally ourselves or discipling them and getting them into a Church so they can be water baptized.

There should be signs and wonders following us. We should be living our lives in light of eternity even though we are living in the present. Jesus gave us authority to cast our demons, so we should do it as necessary. We should be speaking in tongues and praying and praising in tongues. We should be praying for the sick, so they are healed. All Christians should be praying that God would use us in these ways. It can only occur if we are communing with God. The only way it is possible is living with God as a priority. He must be our first priority.

Being in the world but not of the world

John 17: 16 They are not of the world even as I am not of the world. 17 Sanctify them by Your truth. Your word is truth. 18 As You sent Me into the world, so I sent them into the world. 19 For their sakes I sanctify Myself, that they also may be sanctified by the truth.

Jesus prayed for us knowing that the earth is beautiful. Technology is fascinating. There are many pleasures we can enjoy in our lives. Although we are to enjoy our lives, we should always keep Jesus as our priority. God is first. Loving God with all our heart, soul, mind and strength. Loving our neighbour as ourselves should compel us to witness to our neighbours (Matthew 22: 37). Although God gives us all things to enjoy, we must never become drunken with things of the earth. Drinking alcohol is not forbidden in the scriptures. God gave the promised land to Moses and to Joshua. There were vineyards planted. Enjoying wine or alcohol is not a sin. To be drunk is a sin. It is clearly stated we should not be drunk. Intoxication of alcohol causes a person to experience an alternate reality. Some people become quiet and subdued. Some become outspoken. Some get loud and obnoxious. All of them are no longer sober or in control of themselves. Their conscience is dulled.

The conscience of a person is not fully functioning when a person is drunk. Some people commit crimes because of it. Some people do things they later regret because of it. Any type of intoxication of things of the earth is not right. All things are for us to enjoy but we must always remember why we are on the earth – to share Jesus. It should be our driving passion. It is not a religious duty. It is a boldness that treasures the people in such a way that we desire all people to know God. It will only come with sincere desire to help people. It is not something we do because we have to like filling a quota. It's something that should be our prime directive because we are Christ's representatives on the earth. The non-Christians are not going to start telling others about salvation or healing or deliverance. The non-Christians are not going to give money to the gospel, so it can be preached all over the earth. We are the people God chose to do it. If we do not do it and become drunk with the pleasures of life – not even sin – just the normal pleasures of life but we do not preach Christ, we will give account for it. God will hold us accountable for every opportunity we had that we could have shared Christ with someone and didn't.

I realize that life is beautiful. The earth has an attraction of beauty of natural wonders such as Niagara Falls, or the Rocky Mountains or the Bay of Fundy. These are 3 beautiful places in my country. There is a joy in seeing these beautiful things and a joy from enjoying them. It is right that we should enjoy our lives. We should always have our mission as our priority – to share the gospel with all people. There is technology available so that there is the highest quality of television or video games or music or all types of entertainment. All of these things are enjoyable. None of them is wrong. If we do not focus on our primary purpose to win people to Christ, we are wasting our lives.

Mark 15: 15 He said to them, "Go into all the world, and preach the gospel to every creature. 16 He who believes and is baptized will be saved. But he who does not believe will be condemned. 17 These signs will accompany those who believe: In My name they will cast out demons; they will speak with new tongues; 18 they will take up serpents; if they drink any deadly thing, it will not hurt them; they will lay hands on the sick, and they will recover."

I enjoy entertainment and I am not against it. Invite a friend to a movie, but always remember Jesus commanded us to share Jesus Christ with all people. Pray for boldness and for wisdom to know how to speak to people so they know it is sincere and that it clearly shows them a true description of Jesus. It should affect our daily lives in prayer, in deeds, in giving.

Praying

Praying for lost loved ones and friends is something we do because we know it will release opportunities for that person to receive Christ. Not all people receive Jesus Christ on the first mention of His name or what He did. The human heart is not always receptive to salvation. I myself can recount several people trying to share Christ with me. I believed I was smarter than they were in my pursuit of Eastern Religions and the occult. I was deceived. Only later in life did I accept the truth of Jesus so that it changed my life. God can send you to share a word with someone that may be as a seed of God's word planted in the people. God can send someone else to speak about Christ to the person. God can keep releasing mercy or grace towards that person until he or she finally accepts Christ (1 Corinthians 3: 16).

Giving to the gospel

Giving the tithe or the first 10% of your income is commanded by God in the scriptures. It began with Abraham and was later spoken to Moses by God for all of Israel (Exodus 22: 29). God promised to rebuke the devourer as we tithe. God promises to bless us as we give to the storehouse or the place that we receive spiritual nourishment. Giving to the gospel is obedience to God. It not only helps to pay the pastors and ministers get salary for their career; it helps feed the hungry; it helps to send missionaries; it helps the scriptures to be translated into the other languages.

Giving also is your spiritual obedience to God which releases blessings upon your life. It breaks any covetousness off your life. By giving, you show God that you are a wise steward. By giving, you free yourself from the yoke of love of money (which is a sin). By giving, you spread the gospel north, south, east and west. Giving to the gospel is a way for us to help accomplish the great commission. Not all of us get the chance to go to Mozambique or to other parts of Africa or China; we can be partakers of the blessings of those who do go though by giving financially to them. Giving to those who are certainly doing what Jesus commanded, to preach to all people groups in the languages of the nations, is being done by millions of Christians on earth. We should partner with those we can align ourselves with.

There is no way you could give to every ministry or every need. It is a hard truth and one that can overwhelm someone sensitive to giving or caring. This truth was taught to me by God before I became a Christian. I was praying to God, but I did not know God. I was moved with compassion after seeing large numbers of birds trying to get worms or seeds from cement and gravel. I was in the core of Detroit and there was almost no grass or trees. There were birds trying to get seeds or worms from a cement parking lot. I was moved with compassion as in my job I often had to sit with that view as my main focus each day. I would go and buy loaves of whole grain bread and tear it into pieces and each day I gave something. I believed it was good. I would watch them pecking and flying with crumbs. One day, God showed me that a whole flock twice the size came and there wasn't enough. Immediately I thought I would buy more. God let me know there will always be a need that I cannot reach, a people I cannot reach no matter how much I give. It is humbling. It requires dependency on God to provide and faithfulness in giving. It is the effect of the sin of Adam. There never would have been lack if Adam and Eve had not sinned.

Matthew 26: 11 For you have the poor always with you, but you do not always have Me.

There is no way I can give to all the charities I know about or see advertised, nor should I. Even if I were a billionaire, there will always be more people or more needs than any person can ever meet. We should pray for wisdom about the places we give. You tithe to your storehouse or the place that you receive spiritual nourishment. It is usually your church. Sometimes it is some other type of ministry. Knowing that you cannot meet all the needs should compel us to action rather than complacency. I can do something though. I can improve things for someone though. I can help others in a small way. If all Christians had the attitude of giving something to make a difference, there would be less unreached people. There would be less people with needs. Give what you can in faith, believing that God will help others through the giving. Try to give above the tithe. Let God use you as a giver to finance the preaching of the gospel.

Malachi 3 : 10 Bring all the tithes into the storehouse, that there may be food in My house, and test Me now in this, says the Lord of Hosts, if I will not open for you the windows of heaven and pour out for you a blessing, that there will not be room enough to receive it. 11 I will rebuke the devourer for your sakes, so that it will not destroy the fruit of your ground, and the vines in your field will not fail to bear fruit, says the Lord of Hosts. 12 Then all the nations will call you blessed, for you will be a delightful land, says the Lord of Hosts.

Living the Word

Jesus talked about our deeds in his parable of the judgement of the nations. Jesus is the just and righteous judge. All will be gathered, and all will believe they knew God. But some of them such as the goats, will have not lived by doing what they could to share Christ with people in practical ways. Jesus literally talks about feeding people, caring for the poor, caring for those in prison, caring for those who are strangers or ill or without clothing. Literally practical things such as food, clothing, shelter, compassion, and caring.

Giving should be part of our lives not because we must, but because we care. If we do not care about those with these types of needs, we must repent and ask God to forgive us and to soften our hearts. If we do not care for people and we believe we are Christians, we are deceived. Part of the joys of salvation is how you care for others. God gives you the same special unconditional love He has for you, for other people. It is that love shown practical ways that we help others that releases joy in us, and in them thanksgiving towards God. We may be a witness of mercy to people who don't know God and we may be the only ones they meet that are Christians. We should not let such an opportunity pass without doing something. To give somethings with kinds words and possibly a scripture is doing something. God can bless it. Caring for others is a sign of being a Christian.

Matthew 25: 31 "When the Son of Man comes in His glory, and all the holy angels with Him, then He will sit on the throne of His glory. 32 Before Him will be gathered all nations, and He will separate them one from another as a shepherd separates his sheep from the goats. 33 He will set the sheep at His right hand, but the goats at the left.

34 "Then the King will say to those at His right hand, 'Come, you blessed of My Father, inherit the kingdom prepared for you since the foundation of the world. 35 For I was hungry and you gave Me food, I was thirsty and you gave Me drink, I was a stranger and you took Me in. 36 I was naked and you clothed Me, I was sick and you visited Me, I was in prison and you came to Me.'

37 "Then the righteous will answer Him, 'Lord, when did we see You hungry and feed You, or thirsty and give You drink? 38 When did we see You a stranger and take You in, or naked and clothe You? 39 And when did we see You sick or in prison and come to You?'

40 "The King will answer, 'Truly I say to you, as you have done it for one of the least of these brothers of Mine, you have done it for Me.'

41 "Then He will say to those at the left hand, 'Depart from Me, you cursed, into the eternal fire, prepared for the devil and his angels. 42 For I was hungry and you gave Me no food, I was thirsty and you gave Me no drink, 43 I was a stranger and you did not take Me in, I was naked and you did not clothe Me, I was sick and in prison and you did not visit Me.'

44 "Then they also will answer Him, 'Lord, when did we see You hungry or thirsty or a stranger or naked or sick or in prison, and did not serve You?'

45 "He will answer, 'Truly I say to you, as you did it not for one of the least of these, you did it not for Me.'

46 "And they will go away into eternal punishment, but the righteous into eternal life."

Giving

The only difference between the sheep and the goats in the parable is that Some did give to the people they saw that were needy and some did not. Jesus was saying that by giving to the poor who could never repay you, you are directly giving to God because God cares for all people. Although both the sheep and goats knew about Jesus, only the sheep in the parable gave to the needy. Jesus was saying that only those who truly lived the gospel by their works, by their giving, as well as believing in Christ were really the Christians. Faith is only shown by demonstration of works of charity or compassion.

The Faithful or the Unfaithful Servant

God notices what we do with our resources and how we care for our resources. It means we should be wise stewards or servants within our homes. We should properly care for things and teach our children to manage their talents, possessions and time wisely. Jesus gives us an example of a servant who is doing well and of someone who is squandering his life and not working as he should. We will all give account for the spheres of authority in our lives. The things we have we are to care for properly; the people in our life, we should enjoy but also care for deeply; the tasks and jobs we have, we should do them with excellence.

Matthew 25; 45 "Who then is a faithful and wise servant, whom his master has made ruler over his household to give them food at the appointed time? 46 Blessed is that servant whom his master will find so doing when he comes. 47 Truly, I say to you that he will make him ruler over all his goods. 48 But if that evil servant says in his heart, 'My master delays his coming,' 49 and begins to strike his fellow servants and eat and drink with the drunkards, 50 the master of that servant will come on a day when he does not look for him and in an hour he is not aware of 51 and will cut him in pieces and appoint him his portion with the hypocrites, where there shall be weeping and gnashing of teeth.

Luke 21: 34 "Take heed to yourselves, lest your hearts become burdened by excessiveness and drunkenness and anxieties of life, and that Day comes on you unexpectedly. 35 For as a snare it will come on all those who dwell on the face of the whole earth. 36 Therefore watch always and pray that you may be counted worthy to escape all these things that will happen and to stand before the Son of Man."

There will be some who are always ready should the Lord come to gather us because they are living their lives wholly unto God now. There will be those who are not ready. It is essential that we as Christians keep our priorities clear. This means we should do our jobs with excellence. We should do what is best for our customers and our place of business. It means that in our private lives, we should place the gospel first; getting the message of Christ to all people is necessary because Jesus coming. We will give account for our lives.

Jesus gives us the example to show us that all the virgins knew the Lord was coming. They were waiting for his coming. Only five of them were ready though. In the parable of the ten virgins, Jesus emphasizes the wisdom of the wise virgins. When the foolish virgins tried to get oil from them, the wise virgins knew they could not give it or they themselves would not have enough oil.

Matthew 25: The Parable of the Ten Virgins

1 "Then the kingdom of heaven shall be like ten virgins, who took their lamps and went out to meet the bridegroom. 2 Five of them were wise and five were foolish. 3 Those who were foolish took their lamps, but took no oil with them. 4 But the wise took jars of oil with their lamps. 5 While the bridegroom delayed, they all rested and slept.

6 "But at midnight there was a cry, 'Look, the bridegroom is coming! Come out to meet him!'

7 "Then all those virgins rose and trimmed their lamps. 8 But the foolish said to the wise, 'Give us some of your oil, for our lamps have gone out.'

9 "The wise answered, 'No, lest there not be enough for us and you. Go rather to those who sell it, and buy some for yourselves.'

10 "But while they went to buy some, the bridegroom came, and those who were ready went in with him to the wedding banquet. And the door was shut.

11 "Afterward, the other virgins came also, saying, 'Lord, Lord, open the door for us.'
12 "But he answered, 'Truly I say to you, I do not know you.'

13 "Watch therefore, for you know neither the day nor the hour in which the Son of Man is coming.

The wise virgins had their lamps trimmed and had oil with them. The foolish virgins had to return to get oil. They were not ready. The point is that we must always live ready. If we truly live our lives as unto God, giving our very best in our jobs, our families, our communities and relationships, we will be ready for the LORD to come at any minute. Those who missed the coming of the Bridegroom, knew about him but do not prepare.

Should I compare this to the rapture, some will know about Jesus but may be living in willful sin. Those people may be left behind in the rapture. We should keep our hearts right with God each day not only on Sundays and church days. It is an inward dedication of all your life to God.

Spheres of authority

It is important for us to know our gifts and talents and how we can use them to give God glory. Knowing, using developing our talents and gifts and all resources of our lives makes us wise stewards ready for the coming of the LORD. Each person has a circle or authority including family, friends, work associates, customers, businesses we use: education, health care services, technology, media, entertainment, business and economics, arts, government and leadership, and The Christian Church. These spheres of authority give us opportunity to reach people in society in a unique way. We don't have to wait for church to pray for people. If there is someone in a business or public place that requires prayer or healing, we can pray right there. We can help them in all ways possible. We should be leaders in giving assistance to people in need in all spheres of authority of our lives.

The Parable of the Talents

Jesus gives us the parable of the talents or minas or money, The man entrusted goods to them. He gave 5 talents to one; 2 talents to one; one talent to one. Because he is the master, he can decide what to give each person; it also shows delegation based on difference spheres of authority. The one with the most had the most responsibility but they all had some responsibility. The master was going to return, and they would give account of what they did with the talents.

The one with the 5 talents was productive and doubled his talents, as was the one with 2 talents. The one with one talent was fearful and unbelieving and had a bad attitude about his master. He hid it in the ground. He gave him back exactly what was given to him.   master commends the servants who multiply their money but takes away the one talent from the person who was fearful and of poor character.

Matthew 25: 14 "Again, the kingdom of heaven is like a man traveling into a far country, who called his own servants and entrusted his goods to them. 15 To one he gave five talents,[a] to another two, and to another one, to every man according to his ability. And immediately he took his journey. 16 He who had received the five talents went and traded with them and made another five talents. 17 So also, he who had received two gained another two. 18 But he who had received one went and dug in the ground and hid his master's money.

19 "After a long time the master of those servants came and settled accounts with them. 20 He who had received five talents came and brought the other five talents, saying, 'Master, you entrusted to me five talents. Look, I have gained five talents more.'

21 "His master said to him, 'Well done, you good and faithful servant. You have been faithful over a few things. I will make you ruler over many things. Enter the joy of your master.'

22 "He who had received two talents also came and said, 'Master, you entrusted me with two talents. See, I have gained two more talents besides them.'

23 "His master said to him, 'Well done, you good and faithful servant. You have been faithful over a few things. I will make you ruler over many things. Enter the joy of your master.'

24 "Then he who had received the one talent came and said, 'Master, I knew that you are a hard man, reaping where you did not sow, and gathering where you did not winnow. 25 So I was afraid, and went and hid your talent in the ground. Here you have what is yours.'

26 "His master answered, 'You wicked and slothful servant! You knew that I reap where I have not sown, and gather where I have not winnowed. 27 Then you ought to have given my money to the bankers, and at my coming I should have received what was my own with interest.

28 " 'So take the talent from him, and give it to him who has ten talents. 29 For to everyone who has will more be given, and he will have an abundance. But from him who has nothing, even what he has will be taken away. 30 And throw the unprofitable servant into outer darkness, where

there will be weeping and gnashing of teeth.'

Wise Stewards

In the same way that the stewards had to give account for how they spent their talents, God will require that we give account of how we used our talents, gifts, finances, resources, friendships, relationships etc. All things we are given are given to us by God. In all aspects of life, we should use all in our authority to share Christ and to show caring and loving of people. It matters that we develop our gifts; we can improve ourselves. Not all people have the same gifts, but we all have some such as music, art, crafts, sports etc. We should be examples for Christ using these talents. You can enjoy sports and you can show godly character to those around you and perhaps share Christ with them in a unique way. God wants us to enjoy our gifts and talents; he also wants us to naturally – supernaturally care for the people we meet.

2 Corinthians 5: 10 For we must all appear before the judgment seat of Christ, that each one may receive his recompense in the body, according to what he has done, whether it was good or bad.

Remember that the disciples were common people, like fisherman and labourers. God can use us no matter what our career or our hobbies and interests. He can use us because of them to reach people who might never be reached for Christ.

The Rapture

There is special mention that Jesus will appear to all those who are expecting him. That means that as Christians we should be expecting his return.

2 Tim 4: 8 From now on a crown of righteousness is laid up for me, which the Lord, the righteous Judge, will give me on that Day, and not only to me but also to all who have loved His appearing.

If we truly seek God, God promises that we will find him. It means we should be in communication with God regularly. It means that if someone is truly searching for God, that person God will connect with. I know the truth of it myself. I was searching for God truly. I was not searching Christianity but Eastern Religions and the occult. I would never have found God the way I was searching. God sent someone to share the gospel with me. God answered my heart's desire by His mercy revealing Himself to me as Jesus, my Saviour and Lord.

God has promised that all people who truly seek Him will find Him. The Jewish people who truly want to know Messiah will receive Jesus Christ. God will gather them to Israel and Jerusalem.

Jeremiah 29: 13 You shall seek Me and find Me, when you shall search for Me with all your heart. 14 I will be found by you, says the Lord, and I will turn away your captivity and gather you from all the nations and from all the places where I have driven you, says the Lord, and I will bring you back into the place from where I caused you to be carried away captive.

The scriptures say that we will see Jesus one who "was pierced" and they will know Jesus as Saviour and LORD. He will return in his resurrected body not as a spirit only. People will behold Him. Jesus appearance will not be in a Spirit form only; we will literally see the nail prints in the hands and feet. We will recognize him.

Revelation 1: 4 John, To the seven churches which are in Asia:
Grace to you and peace from Him who is and who was and who is to come and from the seven Spirits who are before His throne, 5 and from Jesus Christ, who is the faithful witness, the firstborn from the dead, and the ruler of the kings of the earth. To Him who loved us and washed us from our sins in His own blood, 6 and has made us kings and priests to His God and Father, to Him be glory and dominion forever and ever. Amen.

7 Look! He is coming with clouds,
    and every eye will see Him,
even those who pierced Him.
    And all the tribes of the earth will mourn because of Him.
Even so, Amen.

8 "I am the Alpha and the Omega, the Beginning and the End," says the Lord, "who is and who was and who is to come, the Almighty."
The Rapture will impact the earth.

Those of us living for God each day will expect Him to come as He promised, especially as we notice these signs that he gave us are coming to pass. We will know the season of his coming is near. It should give us urgency in preaching the gospel but also in living righteously and truly loving the people in our lives. Those who have already died and those of us living will be raised together in an instant to be with Jesus in the rapture. We will rise up into the air. We will never be separated from God. This truth brings comfort to Christians who have lost believing family members or loved ones, that we might see them again at the Rapture and during the miliarial reign.

1 Thessalonians 4: 13 But I would not have you ignorant, brothers, concerning those who are asleep, that you may not grieve as others who have no hope. 14 For if we believe that Jesus died and arose again, so God will bring with Him those who sleep in Jesus. 15 For this we say to you by the word of the Lord, that we who are alive and remain until the coming of the Lord will not precede those who are asleep. 16 For the Lord Himself will descend from heaven with a shout, with the voice of the archangel, and with the trumpet call of God. And the dead in Christ will rise first. 17 Then we who are alive and remain shall be caught up together with them in the clouds to meet the Lord in the air. And so we shall be forever with the Lord. 18 Therefore comfort one another with these words.

End of Chapter Questions:

1. Write your priorities (choose 5-6) that you should be an excellent steward over.
2. Explain what it means to be in the world but not of the world.
3. Describe how a Christian's life should show his or her faith: give at least 3 ways.

7 CONCLUSION

In the study of scripture in this book, we have examined main signs of Jesus Christ's return to the earth as he promised he would. Each of the signs was described with scripture. The main focus of the book is to cause awareness of the signs to help God's people discern the season.

1. Signs in the earth – earthquakes, hurricanes, storms etc.
2. Signs in the heavens
3. False Prophets and false Christs
4. Global Revival
5. Worldwide peace
6. Worldwide war
7. Rising to power of one who claims to be God
8. What things a Christian should be doing knowing the end of the age is near
9. Rapture of the Church

The Christians who recognize the signs of Jesus coming will be living exemplary lives because they want to shine as lights in the earth. There is a need for apostles, prophets, evangelists, pastors and teachers to be training up all members of the Church to preach the gospel in all nations of the earth in every language of all the peoples of the earth. Consider yourself and how you might give towards the gospel prayerfully, financially, by volunteering, by going on missionary trips or in other ways.

The prompting to write this book is to speak truth of the origin of sin and its curse to Christians who may be wondering why God is allowing terrible things in the earth; to emphasize the need for prayer and discernment; to know the Biblical evidence of signs of Jesus coming; to prepare our hearts and lives in the present to live in light of eternity with God's message of salvation as a priority in our lives. Please be encouraged to live your best life by faith in Jesus Christ. Be a living witness of His mercy and his glory. Share your faith with unsaved loved ones. Take note of things in the news and pray about them. Pray for discerning of spirits and keep praying for it.

Thank God for strengthening you. Pray for boldness to shine as a light in your life that attracts people to Christ.

1 John 5: 4 for whoever is born of God overcomes the world, and the victory that overcomes the world is our faith. 5 Who is it that overcomes the world, but the one who believes that Jesus is the Son of God?

8 PRAYERS

PRAYERS

The following prayers are samples of prayers you could pray for important reasons. You could pray the same meaning in your own words. The prayers are meant as examples only.

PRAYER FOR SALVATION

Thank you- Jesus that you died for me on the cross. Thank you that you rose from the dead and ascended into heaven. Thank you that you are coming back again. I thank you Jesus for forgiving my sins. Thank you for your blood that cleanses me from all sin and unrighteousness. Thank you that your blood makes me holy. Thank you for saving me. Fill me with the Holy Spirit to overflowing. I pray for the baptism of the Holy Spirit. Lead me to other people who love you and serve you and that can help me know more about you. Give me the discerning of spirits strong. I thank you and praise you. With my mouth, I confess Jesus Christ is my LORD. Amen.

PRAYER FOR BAPTISM OF THE HOLY SPIRIT

Thank you- Jesus that you promised to send the gift of the Holy Spirit to us. Thank you that this promise is to all believers. I am a believer. I want all of you that you will give me. I want to know you God. Baptize me in the Holy Spirit with the evidence of speaking in other tongues. I believe you want to fill me to overflowing with your Spirit so that I might be an effective witness for Christ on the earth. Thank you for saving me. Thank you for your Holy presence. [begin praising God for what He has done for you – sing worship choruses and praise God in your natural language. Believe that He is present with you – start praising and worshipping Him. As phrases come to you in other tongues, say them – praise God with new tongues.] I praise you. I thank you. I receive the baptism of the Holy Spirit.

PRAYER FOR RELEASING ANGELS

God, I thank you that angels are ministering spirits sent as ministers to us. I pray over my prayer request NAME IT HERE. God I pray release angels to perform it. I thank you for releasing the answer to me. I praise you for it. Amen.

PRAYER FOR RESISTING EVIL

I am the redeemed of the LORD. Jesus Christ has saved me. I am a new creation in Christ Jesus. Jesus blood covers me. I live in the spirit. The Holy Spirit of God fills my spirit. O Holy Spirit quicken me; give me wisdom. Pray [expecting God will give you discerning of spirits so you will have the right words to speak.]

In the name of Jesus Christ, I bind you. I rebuke you evil spirit. In the name of Jesus, I command you to go out. You have no place in my life. I cast you out. You have no place with me. I am covered by the blood of Jesus and His righteousness is my righteousness. Go out evil spirit in the name of Jesus Christ!

Thank you, Holy Spirit for your holy presence. Release angels to drive out the enemy. Thank you. Amen.

PRAYER FOR PROTECTION

Holy Spirit release angels to protect me. I plead the blood of Jesus over me. I pray the protection you promise to your people. Cover me Jesus. Holy Spirit give me wisdom, discernment and understanding. Thank you for angels that guard over me. Thank you for your blood that protects me and a hedge of protection around me. I praise you O God. [praise God with some worship choruses and expect God's holy presence to be manifest in you]. Thank you. O God for protection.

PRAYER FOR HEALING

Lord Jesus, Thank you that you gave your life for me so that I can be saved, healed and delivered. I thank you for the scripture that by your stripes I am healed. I thank you for my healing.

NAME THE DISEASE I bind you in the name of Jesus. I cast you out. I pray over myself that I would be whole spirit, soul and body.

Thank you, God. for your healing manifestation in my life. I give you all the glory. Amen.

PRAYER OF REPENTENCE

Jesus, thank you for your blood shed for me. I repent of the sin of NAME IT. I thank you for liberty from sin. I cut off the root of iniquity in my family. I thank you for your empowering presence to live a Holy life. Holy Spirit lead and guide me in the paths of righteousness. Thank you for giving me godly desires. Let my life align with your word. In Jesus name. Amen.

Prayer of dedication as a giver

God, thank you for prospering me. Let me be a giver you can use to give to others. God let my character be humble and giving so that you place things and wealth in my hands and I will give as you lead me. If you prosper me with more than enough, I will obey your promptings to give to the gospel, to people and for the glory of God. Use me as a giver. I give myself wholly to you. In Jesus name. Amen.

OTHER BOOKS BY
CHRIS A. LEGEBOW

Available on Amazon.ca Amazon.com or Kindle
Or the Create Space webstore.

By Living Word Publishers

Angels: Ministering Spirits

An Excellent Spirit: Living Life Wholly Unto God

Covenant With God: God's Relationship With Man

Discovering and Using your Spiritual Gifts

Divine Healing in the Scriptures: God's Mercy Towards Man

Kinds of Giving: From the Holy Scriptures

Signs of Jesus Coming

Spheres of Authority: Know yours

The Commandments

The Doctrine of Christ: Essential Truths of Scripture

The Five-Fold Ministry: Gifts to the Church

Kinds of Prayer. Knowing Them and Using Them Effectively

Living Life Fully: Knowing your Purpose

The Anointing: the Glory of God

The High Calling: Life Worth Living

The Sacraments: A Charismatic Guide

ABOUT THE AUTHOR

Chris Legebow is a Christian Professor of English and Communications. She has taught at the elementary, high school and College and University levels. She has ministered in her local churches in intercessory prayer, teaching Sunday school and other Christian Doctrine classes to children and youth. She has preached to congregations and given her testimony. Although she was not raised in a Christian home, she came to know Jesus Christ as her Saviour and LORD while she was studying in University. This radically transformed her life in terms of priorities and commitment.

She has a strong passion for the great commission – that Jesus Christ would be preached throughout all the earth believing that it a major sign of the LORD's return. She has been a part of several different types of full gospel charismatic churches but has also gained much of her insight and enlightenment from Christian Media and broadcasting. She hopes to continue ministering, serving, interceding and giving and teaching until the LORD returns.

www.ingramcontent.com/pod-product-compliance
Lightning Source LLC
Chambersburg PA
CBHW021221020426
42331CB00003B/409